People of the Bible

The Bible through stories and pictures

Jesus Begins His Work

Copyright © in this format Belitha Press Ltd., 1982

Text copyright © Catherine Storr 1982

Illustrations copyright © Chris Molan 1982

Art Director: Treld Bicknell

First published in the United States of America 1982
by Raintree Publishers Inc.
310 West Wisconsin Avenue, Milwaukee, Wisconsin 53203
in association with Belitha Press Ltd., London.

Conceived, designed and produced by Belitha Press Ltd.,
2 Beresford Terrace, London N5 2DH

ISBN 0-8172-1978-1 (U.S.A.)

Library of Congress Cataloging in Publication Data

Storr, Catherine.
   Jesus begins his work.

   (People of the Bible)
   Summary: A simple retelling of the New Testament
stories of the first miracles performed by Jesus and of
his calling of his twelve Apostles.
      1. Jesus Christ—Biography—Juvenile literature.
2. Bible. N.T.—Biography—Juvenile literature.
3. Christian biography—Palestine—Juvenile literature.
[I. Jesus Christ—Biography. 2. Bible stories—N.T.]
I. Molan, Christine, ill. II. Title. III. Series.
BT302.S878   1982   226'.09505   82-9037

ISBN 0-8172-1978-1   AACR2

4 5 6 7 8 9 10 11 12 13 14   98 97 96 95 93 92 91 90 89 88

Jesus Begins His Work

RETOLD BY CATHERINE STORR
PICTURES BY CHRIS MOLAN

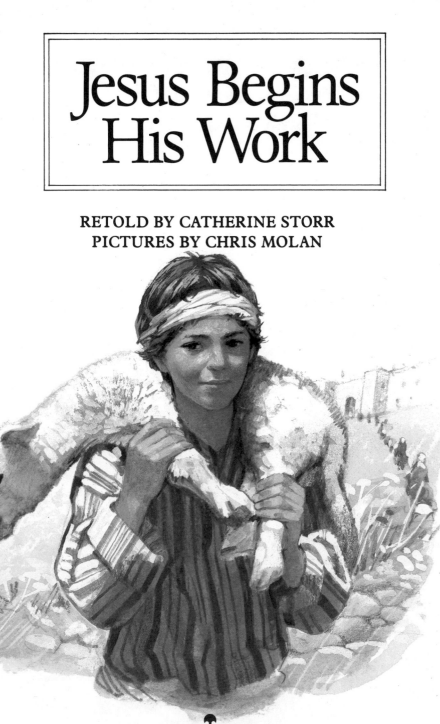

Raintree Childrens Books
Milwaukee
Belitha Press Limited • London

Every year Mary and Joseph used to go to Jerusalem for the feast of the Passover. When Jesus was twelve years old, he went with them.

When the feasting was over, Mary and Joseph started on the long journey back to Nazareth. Jesus wasn't with them. They thought he was traveling with some other friends and relatives.

It wasn't until the end of the first day that they discovered he had been left behind.

Joseph and Mary had to go back to Jerusalem. They looked everywhere for Jesus. At last they found him in the Temple. He was talking to the wise teachers there, asking questions, and answering them too.

Mary said to him, "How could you do this to us? We've been terribly worried about you."

Jesus said, "Don't you know I have to do what God tells me?"

But he went back to Nazareth with Joseph and Mary and did what he was told.

Many years later, John the Baptist, a cousin of Jesus, was living in the wilderness. He taught people to share their clothes and food with others.

He said to them, "I am not the greatest prophet. But he is coming soon. I have seen him and I know he is the son of God."

One day, John was with two of his followers, Andrew and Simon Peter. He saw Jesus coming and he said, "Look! There is the son of God."

When Andrew heard this, he left John and followed Jesus. He said to his brother, Simon Peter, "Come and see. We have found Christ, our leader."

Jesus said, "Follow me!"

Soon after this Jesus found Philip, who followed him too. All these men were called the disciples of Jesus.

As well as Andrew and Simon Peter and Philip, there were James and John the sons of Zebedee, Matthew and Bartholomew, Thomas and Simon, James the son of Alphaeus, Thaddeus, and Judas Iscariot.

One day there was a great wedding party
in a village called Cana. Mary and Jesus
and his disciples had been invited.

But when they arrived at the feast, all the
wine was gone.

Mary said to Jesus, "There's no more wine for the guests to drink. Is there anything you can do?"

She said to the servants, "Whatever my son tells you, you should do."

Jesus told the servants to fill six big jars with water. Then he said, "Pour something to drink from the jars, and take it to the master of the house."

As they did this, they saw that the water had turned into wine, and it was even better than the wine they had drunk before.

This was Jesus' first miracle.

After this Jesus did many more miracles. He made ill people better.

Once when he was teaching in a house full of people, a man who couldn't stand or walk was lowered on his bed through the roof into the middle of the house.

Jesus said to him, "Take up your bed and walk." The man found that he could do as he was told. He was cured.

Another time, a blind man was brought to Jesus. Jesus spat on some earth and rubbed it on the man's eyes. Then he asked, "What do you see?"

The man said, "I see men, like trees, but walking." He could see again.

One day, a ruler of the synagogue, called Jairus, came to see Jesus and said, "My little daughter is dying. Please save her."

Jesus went to Jairus' house and found everyone there crying and wailing. He said, "Don't be sad. The little girl isn't dead, she's only asleep." He went inside and took her by the hand and said, "Get up!"

The little girl stood up, alive and well.

Jesus said, "Give her some food, and let's keep it a secret."

Jesus and his disciples traveled to many places. They took no money or food, and they taught people who came to listen to them.

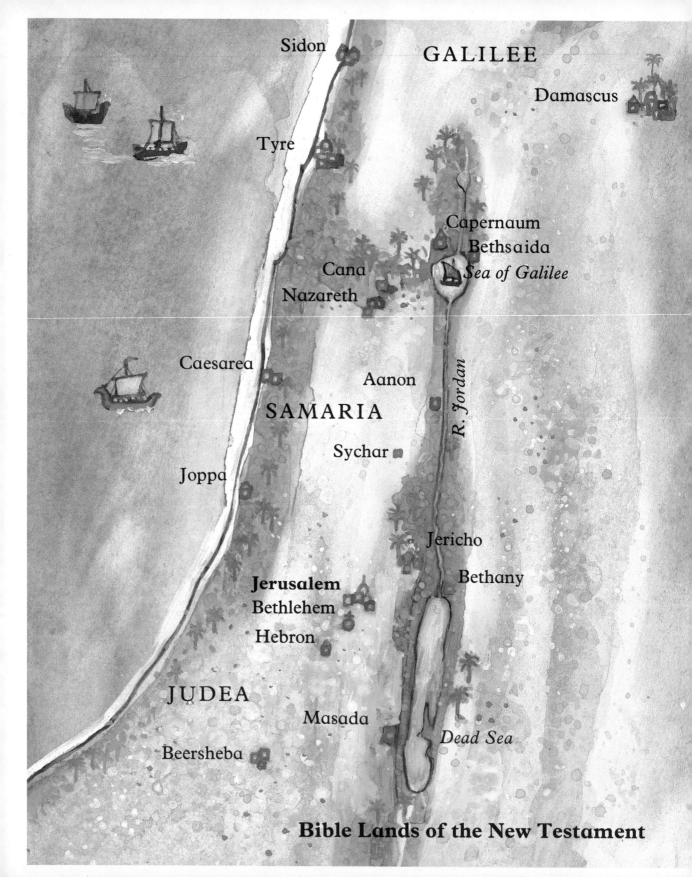

Bible Lands of the New Testament